PICTURES

LINDA AKSOMITIS

Published by Pearson Education Limited, Edinburgh Gate, Harlow, Essex, CM20 2JE
Registered company number: 872828

www.pearsonschools.co.uk

First published by Pearson
a division of Pearson New Zealand Ltd
67 Apollo Drive, Rosedale, North Shore 0632, New Zealand
Associated companies throughout the world

Text © Pearson 2010

Page Layout: Ruby-Anne Fenning
Cover Design and Illustrations: Sarah Healey

The right of Linda Aksomitis to be identified as author of this work has been
asserted by her in accordance with the Copyright, Designs and Patents Act 1988.

First published 2010
This edition published 2012

2022
10

British Library Cataloguing in Publication Data
A catalogue record for this book is available from the British Library

ISBN 978-0-43507-574-3

Printed and bound in Great Britain by Ashford Colour Press Ltd.

Acknowledgements
We would like to thank the children and teachers of Bangor Central Integrated
Primary School, NI; Bishop Henderson C of E Primary School, Somerset; Brookside
Community Primary School, Somerset; Cheddington Combined School,
Buckinghamshire; Cofton Primary School, Birmingham; Dair House Independent
School, Buckinghamshire; Deal Parochial School, Kent; Lawthorn Primary School,
North Ayrshire; Newbold Riverside Primary School, Rugby and Windmill Primary
School, Oxford for their invaluable help in the development and trialling of the Bug
Club resources.

Every effort has been made to contact copyright holders of material reproduced in
this book. Any omissions will be rectified in subsequent printings if notice is given
to the publishers.

A division of Pearson New Zealand Ltd

CONTENTS

Sam Christos pointed the camera and peered at its screen. The tiny square filled with the miniature lake, miniature black spruce, miniature jack pine, even more miniature . . . What? What *was* that? He blinked, moved his nose closer to the images, stared. Though it was still a long way away, it was a . . . *gigantic* shadow. A creature tucked between the trees.

Was it a bear? Should he run? No. Whatever it was, he had to have a picture to show Grandpa. His finger shot forward, covered the silver button ready to snap a picture.

The thought crossed his mind – what if it *was* a bear? Worse yet, what if it was something bigger and wilder and meaner? Hands trembling, he carefully pushed the button halfway down to focus the camera. This couldn't turn out blurry.

Another second.

The shadow creature didn't move.

Sam dared to take a breath and watched the image fuzz, focus and clear. The camera was ready. Under his fingertip, the button went down all the way and clicked.

"Did you get me?" It was a girl's voice. Yelling. Where had she come from? And what was she doing diving into his picture?

Sam's eyes left the camera and looked up to see a girl racing towards him through the trees. The shadowy creature had disappeared. At least he didn't have to worry about what kind of animal it had been.

The captured photo was frozen on the camera's screen – he had ten seconds to stare at it and fume. There she was in the foreground, long black hair flying, pink shorts, bright orange feet airborne in a jump. Only bits and pieces of the shadow creature stuck out around her.

"Did you get me?" she shouted again, closer now.

Sam's fear of a moment ago turned to frustration. He'd like to erase her from the picture and the forest in front of him.

"I've been doing gymnastics. Could you tell? I thought about ballet, too, but there aren't any classes for it around here. Maybe the next place we live will have some."

Sam groaned. His picture was ruined. And along with it his opportunity to take a nature photo that would show Grandpa what a great photographer he could be. It was all her fault.

Sam refused to look up as she approached, but the dried-up bits of pine cones crunching under her stomping feet told him exactly where she was. Somewhere high in the trees a raven squawked at her, like a teacher sending her off to the principal's office for what she'd done.

"Yes, unfortunately I got you," said Sam when she stopped beside him.

She grabbed his arm and peered at the camera. "Picture's gone already. Can I see it?"

"You ruined my picture, you know."

"Oh . . . Can't you just take another?" She twirled and pointed towards the towering green spruce behind her. "Doesn't your camera hold tons of pictures? There's room for 500 on my grandmère's."

Sam opened his mouth to speak, then hesitated. How could he tell her he'd seen a shadow creature? What if she just laughed? Maybe she wasn't scared of bears, even if it had been one. Before he told anyone – especially her – he'd have to make sure some of the animal showed in the picture once it was downloaded onto Grandpa's computer.

The girl didn't wait for an answer. Instead, her mouth opened and more words toppled out. "I'm Taneal Mercredi. Who are you? How long are you staying for?"

"Samuel Christos, but everyone calls me Sam and my grandpa Samuel," he replied automatically, providing the same information he always did on his family's shared annual holiday. They'd all been planning this holiday to Saskatchewan for two years. Now he was picture-hunting on his own and Grandpa was hobbling around with a walker, while Dad and Grandma fussed over him and tried to help him learn how to talk again after his stroke.

And Mum, she'd had to give up the first week of their holidays because the tiny eco-friendly clothing company where she was a buyer was re-organising.

Nothing was going right at all.

Taneal babbled on. "I'm with my dad, but he's working on a big project designing a new video game that has gremlins and weird alien creatures called laplatas – they're kind of like giant lizards, except they can turn on protective armour whenever they want."

"Oh yeah?" said Sam, without much enthusiasm. He didn't want to encourage her. Taneal's dad sounded more interesting than she did. The game might be kind of like the one he played on the Internet after school if he didn't have homework.

A huge mosquito, thirsty as a vampire, drilled into Sam's arm. Swat! He spat on his finger, cleaned the blood up and wiped it on his red hemp shorts – his favourite eco-friendly ones. At least it wouldn't show and upset Grandma, who always seemed to be worried about his messy hair or his dirty shoes or the orange spaghetti sauce stains on his shirt. She was different this year, fussing over everyone.

Sam picked up his things and headed back to the resort, with Taneal in talkative pursuit. "What kind of games do you like? My favourites are the ones where I have to solve things, like in Dad's new game. There's a way you can get armour just like the laplatas."

"Yeah, well don't tell me how," said Sam. "If I play it, I'd like to find the clues myself."

Taneal grinned, then talked on and on and on about how to play the game as they followed the path to Land of the Loon Resort.

Crossing the recreation area, they passed a mini-van backed up to a picnic table, with two noisy little kids running around, squealing, "Hot dogs, hot dogs, we want hot dogs."

"Hi," called Sam, waving. He'd spent a lot of time here this morning, near the beach, before heading off to see what pictures he could get. Then he remembered the shadow creature. He had to download the photos from the camera and see if he could make out any kind of shape around Taneal.

"Hey! Land of the Loon to Sam, are you there?"

Sam suddenly realised that Taneal had stepped in front of him. "Sorry," he muttered. "I was thinking about something."

"I asked how old you are. I'm eleven."

"Eleven, too."

Taneal grabbed his arm and pulled him to a stop. "When's your birthday?" she demanded.

"February 8," he said, glaring down at her hand until she dropped it. A small breeze carried the scent of fish on a barbecue and his stomach rumbled.

"Hey, mine's the seventh," she shouted, bouncing so that the hair hanging halfway down her back flew up around her face. "I'm older than you are! I'm older than you are!"

Sam didn't think one day was worth that kind of a fuss. He walked faster and ignored her. He had to get back.

The door opened in the cabin in front of them, and Dad, his long skinny legs as white and bare as peeled parsnips, stepped out. He let the screen door bang as he dropped a handful of silver tinfoil-wrapped potatoes onto the barbecue.

"That your dad?" asked Taneal. "He looks like you." She giggled.

"My legs are nowhere near as pale as that!" protested Sam. "My dad never gets outside because he sits in front of his computer most of the day writing books. They've got his latest, *Never Sit on a Spider*, at the airport bookstore in Saskatoon."

Sam's dad solved mysteries in his books, and now maybe Sam could solve the mystery of the shadow creature here in Waskesiu.

"Really? Your dad's a real writer!" Taneal's jaw dropped and for a short moment she was silent. "I want to be one, too," she added at last.

The kids Sam knew back home seemed to think being a writer was boring. Sometimes people even made jokes about his dad staying home to be a babysitter and housekeeper while his mother went out to work and earn a living for the family. He'd given up trying to tell them how many hours Dad spent writing every day.

Suddenly, Sam saw a way to get rid of Taneal until her dad's game was ready for testing, and stop her ruining his holidays. "I'm sure Dad would tell you all about writing, maybe even help you write a story or something."

"Oh, wow! That would be great!"

As Sam led Taneal towards their cabin to introduce her to Dad, the camera swung around his neck and smacked against his chest. And his heart pounded right back as he thought about the creature. Would he be able to tell if it was a bear, or something scarier, when he downloaded the pictures? Or would there just be a photo of pesky Taneal?

Grandma was holding the cabin door open now, so that Grandpa could get out. It took him half a dozen halting steps to get past it with his walker. Sam looked away.

The next morning, Sam lay in bed, still feeling disappointed. All that had shown in his photo was Taneal's enormous leap. The bits of dark shadow that stuck out around her hadn't looked like anything at all.

Sam turned over on the narrow twin bed and listened to Dad's snoring. It sounded like the grunting warthog he'd seen at the zoo.

He pulled the patchwork quilt over his head and tried to go back to sleep, but it was no use. He might as well find something to do while the grown-ups slept late.

Outside, it was already warm.

"Hey, Sam!" yelled a voice.

For a moment, Sam thought something exciting might be happening, but it was only Taneal.

She was pushing an old blue bicycle. "The office lady says you can use this bike of theirs if you want. I rode mine over. We can take the trails along Anglin Lake and into Prince Albert National Park. We're just on the edge here."

Sam wasn't the least bit pleased to see Taneal, but the offer of a bike ride tempted him. On a bike, he could follow her at a distance and not have to listen to all that chatter. "Okay. I guess that'd be good."

He took the steps from the deck two at a time, reaching the road and the old blue bicycle just as Taneal wheeled up her own bike. Though the office bike was nothing like his new one back home, the chain, at least, looked oiled and new.

"I can show you a good place near here where there's usually a beaver dam."

Did bears hang out around beaver dams? Sam didn't want to ask. Instead, he said, "Can we be back by the time everyone wakes up?" Grandma had promised to make waffles for breakfast and he didn't want to miss them.

"Sure," she said, climbing onto her bike.

At first the air felt cool, but Sam soon warmed up as he pedalled hard to keep up with Taneal. He had no idea where they were going as they zipped along paths between the cabins, then cycled over narrow hiking trails surrounded by trees and darted across gravel roads.

More twists, more turns. Lots of trees, many with leaves instead of needles. Soon they reached a narrow channel running out from the lake and found the promised beaver lodge poking up out of the shallow water – a metre-high mound of dried grey sticks and twigs stuck together with mud.

Taneal stopped. "This is a good one, but I've seen ones even bigger."

Sam laid his bike on the ground beside the water and pulled out the camera. "Not me." In fact, he'd never seen one up close at all. Snap. Snap. He walked over the spongy ground, trying to get the perfect photo to show Grandpa.

Taneal chattered on, telling him all about beavers and how they lived. She seemed to know a lot.

"Do you know much about other animals?" he asked, clicking back to preview the past five pictures he'd taken. They were pretty good.

"Lots! What do you want to know about? My moushoom – that's my grandpa – he's told me lots about everything: badger, red fox, moose, elk, otter . . ."

"What about bears? Or animals even bigger than bears?"

"Bears *are* the biggest, and the most dangerous."

"That's what I thought," muttered Sam. But

if Taneal was wrong and there was something even bigger than a bear in the forest here, it would surely be even more dangerous.

TWO

Sam poured maple syrup into each perfect square of his waffle, making sure every tiny golden box filled right to the top without overflowing.

"Wow, not even one drip over the edge," said Taneal. Her waffle was swimming in a rich sea of purple syrup she'd brought over to share.

"The next one I'll try your stuff," said Sam. "It'll take three or four waffles to fill me up."

Grandma smiled. "Taneal, this choke cherry syrup your aunt made is delicious."

"I help her pick choke cherries every year," said Taneal between bites. "Them and blueberries, but mostly we make pie and jam from the blueberries. Choke cherries make the best syrup."

When breakfast was finished, Sam asked Grandma if she needed help with the dishes.

"Not today. You and Taneal should go exploring on those bikes. It's holiday time." She glanced at Grandpa, who was using his walker to pull himself up from the couch. "You two go and have some fun."

Sam shot out the door and down the stairs to where the bikes were leaning on the cabin wall. Next door, an old man – maybe as old as Grandpa – was hoisting two large suitcases into the back of his car.

"I sure feel bad for your grandpa," said Taneal. "My moushoom has twenty-two grandchildren and he can still carry the canoe on a portage through the bush when we're out on the river."

"Last year Grandpa could have, too," said Sam quickly. But he didn't really want to talk about it. "How come you only mention your dad and your moushoom? Where's your mother?"

Taneal pushed her bike out slowly, and the early morning sun glinted off its chrome. "My mother died in a car accident in Montreal four years ago, when we lived there." As she turned towards him, a mist over her dark chocolate eyes held a suggestion of tears.

"Oh." Sam didn't know what else to say. Grandpa's stroke didn't seem quite so bad any more. At least he was recovering, even if they couldn't go out taking pictures together. Every day he got a little stronger and a little better at moving around; it was also getting easier for him to speak.

"Where do you want to ride?" Taneal asked.

Sam stared at her, trying to decide what to do. Would she laugh if he told her about the creature? Or would she have some ideas about what it might have been?

"You know," he said hesitantly, "yesterday . . . when you ran into me . . . I was taking a picture of an animal that looked humongous." There, it was out. He pushed down on the bike pedal, anxious to get moving.

"Like a bear?" Taneal brought her bike up even with Sam's.

"I don't know much about bears," Sam said. "But it would have to be a bear . . . or something bigger. All I know is that, even from a long way away, it sure made me feel scared."

"Good idea staying far away then. Moushoom says we have to respect the animals if we want them to respect us. Otherwise, we could end up being lunch!"

"Your moushoom says that?"

"No," replied Taneal with a grin. "*I* say that."

Sam took a deep breath. "I need to get a picture of that creature – whatever it is – for Grandpa."

"Okay, we'll go and look for it," said Taneal. "But we're absolutely, positively, one hundred per cent, sure enough *not* getting close to whatever it is."

"All right!" cheered Sam, lifting both hands from the handlebars and giving a double high-five to Land of the Loon. Still, along with the excitement he felt some twinges of fear. How dangerous would getting this picture be? Would he be sorry when he found the creature?

All morning they pedalled and pedalled and pedalled. Through Anglin Lake village. Around the lake shore. Between dozens of cabins where people waved and called hello. They stopped at a playground for a while, but the only other kids were just babies with their parents.

After lunch they pedalled some more, changed direction and followed some roaring quad bikes down a trail. They pedalled so long and so hard that Sam felt as if he might never be able to pedal again.

He pulled off the trail and flopped on the ground under a spruce tree that seemed to stretch right up to the sky. A pesky fly nearly flew up his nose as he inhaled deeply. The smell here was sort of like the deodorisers Mum bought for their house in the city. It reminded him of yesterday, though they were a lot further from the boat ramp and beach than he'd been when he saw the creature yesterday.

Taneal sat down beside him and took out her water bottle for a drink. "You know, we've been completely around the village and seen lots of people. Nobody's told us to watch out for a bear wandering too close or any other big wild animals."

"That doesn't mean there isn't something around," retorted Sam, though he was also beginning to wonder if yesterday's creature sighting had been a figment of his imagination.

"Animals don't just pop up when you want to see them though. In the winter, when Moushoom and I go out with snowshoes, sometimes we go for kilometres before we see even a single rabbit in the snow."

Sam jumped up. "Of course! The creature is camouflaged in the trees, so we're never going to see it if we just stick to these paths."

"Getting off the path is dangerous," said Taneal.

"But what if that's the only way to see it?"

"Then I guess we won't see it." She got up and stood with her hands on her hips, staring at him.

"What if we just go halfway? You know, off the trail, but not tromping through the forest?"

"With our bikes?"

Sam looked into the trees and shook his head.

"I guess not. It would be easy to walk through the trees here, like it is at Land of the Loon, but the bikes would have trouble running over branches and stuff."

"Tomorrow I can show you a place where the forest is so thick, you can't see into it at all," promised Taneal.

If the forest was as thick as that, reasoned Sam, the creature probably wouldn't be there, but he said "okay" anyway.

He swatted a few more flies, backed away a bit and held up the camera, peering at the world through the miniature screen. As he turned in a slow circle, he caught a suggestion of a shadowy shape away to his left. It wasn't Taneal. Taneal was much closer and to his right.

Sam squinted and put his hand up to shield his eyes from the late afternoon sun. Nothing. There was nothing there. Talking about the creature must have made him imagine it.

"Hey, Sam, how long till you're finished?" called Taneal.

"Just a few more pictures." Sam took a few steps in the opposite direction, held the viewfinder up again and snapped.

He moved the camera, focusing it on a wide tree as far back as he could see. But the tree was only wide for about a quarter of the way up. That was strange. Trees didn't change shape like that.

Then, suddenly, half the tree split away in a giant step.

The creature! It had to be the creature! It was standing motionless again, almost as if it really were part of the forest. It would be hard to get a picture, because of all the other trees between them. How could he let Taneal know so that she didn't move and get in the way again? He waved his hand to catch her attention.

She had sat down to drink, tipping up her water bottle to drain its contents. She hadn't noticed a thing.

Maybe he should just shoot the photo. "Keep steady," he whispered to himself. The silver button felt slippery under his finger as he tried to focus. His finger slipped. Click.

A blurry image appeared on the preview screen. The picture was terrible.

Taneal rose to her knees and looked across at him.

He waved his arm, trying to indicate caution without pointing directly at the creature behind her. What if she shouted again? That would scare it away.

Sam steadied the camera. Maybe Taneal would figure out that he was trying to take a picture just by looking at him.

The camera wasn't ready yet.

Peering at the screen once more, Sam felt his heart sink. Tree by tree, the creature was getting closer to Taneal! It would scare her or, worse, hurt her. Or, even worse . . .

Animals didn't really have people for lunch, did they?

Words of warning caught in Sam's throat and choked him. He found he couldn't yell. He couldn't even breathe.

Taneal was intent on standing her bike up, sliding her water bottle into its carrier. What would she do if he shouted to be careful? Perhaps she'd do something that would make the creature charge right at her?

More seconds passed.

This was all his fault. Taneal was in danger and he couldn't do anything to protect her.

Suddenly, Taneal seemed to realise that Sam had the camera pointed at something. She turned. Her bike dropped, hitting the ground with a thud.

Sam stopped breathing.

Three things happened at exactly the same time: Taneal yelled, the creature disappeared into the shadows of the trees and Sam's finger pressed the camera button.

The camera bounced against Sam's chest as he dropped it and raced towards her.

"What . . . was . . . that?" gasped Taneal.

"I thought you'd know."

Taneal shook her head, glanced into the trees, then back at Sam without saying anything.

Finally, Sam asked, "Are you okay?"

She nodded. "If that's a bear, it's gigantic!"

"Now, do you believe me?"

"Oh yeah!"

They were quiet as they pedalled back, both lost in their own thoughts. Finally, Taneal broke the silence. "Maybe we could see the bear, or whatever it is, more clearly if we were on Anglin Lake?"

It wasn't a bear – Sam was sure of that, even if Taneal wasn't. He had to get a clear picture. Taking it from the lake would be perfect, it wouldn't be dangerous at all. "But how do we get *on* the lake?"

"I'll get Dad to ask if one of my cousins can take us out kayaking tomorrow. Can you swim?" She didn't wait for an answer. "Doesn't matter anyway. We have to wear life jackets in the kayaks."

"Sure, I can swim. Dad and I went swimming at that tiny beach by the boat ramp on our first two days."

When they reached the cabin, Taneal pedalled off home, while Sam hurried inside to download the images. By the time he had everything set up, Dad had arrived back and Grandpa had got up.

Last year, the two of them had looked a lot

alike – same brown hair, same bushy eyebrows, same slight upturned nose, all of which Sam had inherited, too. Then, Grandpa and Dad had both stood straight and tall; now Grandpa slumped over the walker, pushing it along in front of him like a baby who hasn't learned to walk yet.

Grandpa joined him at the laptop. "So what did you get . . . pictures of?"

It hurt Sam to hear Grandpa struggle to find the words to say what he meant. "Lots of things, Grandpa."

Sam used the mouse to scroll through the images, anxious to get to the last one. "Beaver lodge, ravens, some birds' nests, even a fawn."

"Very . . . nice. This one," said Grandpa, pointing at the fifth one of a raven, "has very good . . . balance. The picture is in, in . . . "

"Thirds," guessed Sam, as he stared at the division of blue sky, green trees behind and the raven up close in the foreground. That was one of the last lessons in composition Grandpa had given him a year ago.

Grandpa nodded.

Unable to wait any longer, Sam scrolled through to the last of the images. Click-click. He enlarged it to full screen and stared.

The picture showed a few dozen tall trees and a shadow far back, but it wasn't very clear.

"Let me have . . . the mouse."

"Sure." Sam pushed it towards Grandpa and watched as he opened up the graphics software and began to work.

They didn't need to talk. Sam knew Grandpa was lightening and brightening and sharpening the image to make it stand out. He watched carefully, trying to keep track of the percentages and sequences Grandpa used. Each time Grandpa stopped, Sam nodded, indicating he understood what he had done, just as he used to when they were outside taking pictures. They hadn't spoken a lot then either, since sounds scared away the animals.

"A bear," Grandpa said at last, as he stared at the shadowy picture. "I hoped we'd get . . . pictures of a bear when we planned . . . this trip. I don't have one . . . in our collection."

Sam was sure the animal was much too large

to be a bear, but of course Grandpa wouldn't be able to tell that from a picture. His heart began to beat faster with excitement. What if he could get a picture no one else had got? Sam wanted a picture that would make him famous; a picture that would make Grandpa proud of all the things he'd taught him.

THREE

Taneal's cousin, Billy, was nearly as thin as the braid of black hair that hung down his back, well past his shoulders. His brown eyes twinkled like Taneal's.

"This is a good put-in spot," said Billy, lining up all three kayaks in the grass. "It's shallow out there for a bit, so you'll have time to get things figured out, Sam."

"That's good," said Sam. Looking at the long red kayak, he suddenly felt nervous. It seemed too narrow to hold and balance his weight on the water. Would this be like the first time he tried golf with Grandpa? It had taken him ten swings to hit the ball even a little way.

"Me first, I'm the oldest," said Taneal, grabbing one of the kayaks and pushing it towards the water. "I'll show Sam how to do it."

"Slow down there, Taneal," said Billy. "Let's go through the basics first."

Taneal sighed – a great, noisy sigh that set Sam's teeth on edge. Then, to make matters worse, Dad came down to the shore to watch while Grandpa and Grandma set up lawn chairs further back on the sandy beach and got out the camera to take pictures.

"Ready, Sam?" asked Dad, peering into his face.

He took a deep breath and nodded. "Sure."

Taneal pushed her kayak into the water, put one leg over each side of the cockpit and balanced herself with her paddle while Billy held the kayak still. In one swift motion, she flopped into the seat, pulled her legs in and thrust them forward out of sight.

Billy pointed at the front of the kayak. "Here's the bow and the back is called the stern. Taneal's sitting on the seat in the cockpit, with her legs spread out along the edge like a frog's, feet on the footplate. Got that?"

"Yes," said Sam. The nautical terms were easy

– he'd learned them during the holiday they'd had on a cruise ship.

Taneal wobbled the kayak from side to side. "See, Sam, a kayak's really easy to keep balanced."

"Watch it, Taneal, or you'll be swimming!" Billy held up a paddle with identical white blades on both ends and handed it to Sam. "This paddle's flat, so it doesn't matter how you hold it."

Sam gripped it in front of himself, a hand on each side, imagining how he would use it in the water.

Billy nodded. "Hold it overhand, so your fingers are underneath – and keep both hands the same distance from the blades."

Taneal paddled into the lake and spun around to show Sam how to steer. It looked easy enough.

Billy pushed Sam's kayak into the water and held it while Sam stepped awkwardly over it. The water felt cold at first, as he'd discovered before while swimming, but after a few minutes it was fine.

"Not as warm as a swimming pool, is it?" said Billy with a grin.

The kayak wobbled beneath him as Sam settled lower. It was hard to tell if he was positioned over the seat or not.

"Go, Sam," yelled Grandpa.

"You'll be ready for a race soon," called Taneal, swinging her kayak to face Sam in the water so she could watch what was going on.

Sam dropped into the kayak seat and pulled his legs in awkwardly. The kayak wobbled, but Billy kept it from tipping.

"Here's your waterproof bag with your lunch and camera, Sam," said Billy. "Don't want them getting wet if you go for a swim."

Sam grabbed the large yellow bag and pushed it down beside his legs in the cockpit. He had to keep the camera safe – if he sighted that creature on shore, he needed a picture!

"Once you've got the idea of paddling, we'll take off," said Billy, putting the paddle in his hands. "Give it a try."

Sam dipped the right blade into the water. Nothing happened. He dipped again, this time feeling the resistance of water against the blade as he pulled. The kayak moved! He did it again. Whoops! That made the kayak turn left. He lifted the right-hand blade and dipped the left blade into the water instead, raising a cool splash of water.

Left, right. Left, right. The kayak moved out into the lake. Three more left dips and he could see everyone on shore. He waved and called, "See you later!"

Billy and Taneal swooshed past him to lead the way through the bays around the lake. Overhead, the sun started its climb across the sky in the company of half a dozen different birds – hawks with their black wings spread, squawking white pelicans and the loons for which the resort was named, whose haunting songs had lulled him to sleep each night since they'd arrived. It was a perfect day on the water.

Billy stopped paddling to let Sam catch up. "How's it going?"

"Great! Kayaking is the best thing I've ever done!" And, Sam assured himself, it wasn't just because he hadn't had any trouble figuring out how to paddle. The best part was being on the lake, gliding past the evergreen forest on the shore, dipping his fingers into the crystal clear water, catching sight of long, thin pike jumping out of the water, as if they were also celebrating the amazing day.

Soon, Taneal slowed her pace so she could paddle side by side with Sam. "See there?" She pointed with her paddle. "That's near where we were yesterday when we saw it."

"Keep your eyes open," said Sam, smiling at Taneal. He felt like they were almost partners now, both trying to find out what the creature was and get its picture.

Left, right, left, right, left, right. What was that on shore now? "Do you see that?"

"What?"

Sam pointed with his paddle. "That large shape – it's in front of the trees now, not in them. I'll bet it's the creature!"

Taneal held her hand up to shade her eyes. "Where?"

It disappeared into the trees again.

Sam sighed with frustration as Taneal

paddled her kayak up beside his and reached out to steady it. "Maybe you should get your camera ready."

"Good idea," said Sam, reaching further into the cockpit for the camera bag.

"Stick your paddle under those straps at the front, so you don't drop it in the lake," directed Taneal.

Sam shoved the paddle in place, then leaned forward to pull the bag out. His leg muscles hurt from being stretched out against the kayak's curved sides. He pulled the camera out.

"Billy!" shouted Taneal.

"What?" Billy lifted his paddle and turned his kayak.

"We've stopped so Sam can get some pictures," she called.

"Did you tell Billy about the creature?" Sam asked quietly, as he turned the camera on, keeping as still as he could to avoid rocking the boat.

Billy was paddling back towards them as Taneal shook her head and lowered her voice. "He might tell my dad, and then Dad might say we couldn't look for it any more, whatever it is."

That was the same reason Sam hadn't talked a lot about it with Grandpa either. He and Taneal were being careful, but the grown-ups might still want them to give up on trying to get a photo.

Sam pointed the camera towards the shore, hoping the creature would step out into the sunlight again. He peered at the screen, but the trees were so far away they were just tiny green blobs. He pushed the zoom button to get closer. Nothing much happened. He snapped a picture anyway.

Billy paddled up beside Sam. "Tired yet? We've come three or four kilometres already."

"I'm okay. It's fun." Sam panned the camera across the landscape again. Snap. Snap. Snap.

Behind Billy, something big emerged from the trees on the shore. Was it the creature? Sam glanced across at Taneal.

She pointed to the same spot, where a bit of a clearing led down to the water. "Those trees over there are kind of pretty."

Sam focused the camera again and clicked.

The picture was clear and sharp, but he was so far away. There was no telling until he had the photo downloaded and in full size on the computer screen whether he'd be able to see the creature in it.

While Billy and Taneal steadied the kayak for him, Sam put his camera back in the waterproof bag. "Let's keep paddling."

By the time they pulled the kayaks up on shore for lunch, Sam could barely lift his arms. Yesterday, they'd biked until his legs ached and now his arms felt the same.

"We'll get out of the sun to eat," said Billy.

Sam hadn't realised how hungry he was until he took the first bite of his cheese and lettuce sandwich. He gobbled up both slices of bread, two oatmeal cookies, an orange and Taneal's second granola bar as well.

"Will you tell us some of the stuff you say when you're a guide for tourists?" Taneal asked her cousin.

Billy shrugged. "I just tell them about some of the plants, trees, birds and stuff."

Sam had been thinking about closing his eyes for a rest, but he was wide awake as soon as Billy started talking. He took more pictures of the things Billy was pointing out, along with a few video clips, so he could remember it all to show Grandpa. Even if he didn't have a good picture of the creature, at least he'd have something to share.

Finally, Billy said, "We'd better head back. Weather's changing." He pointed at the rolling dark clouds that had appeared on the horizon. "Gather up everything, especially the rubbish. We take back everything we brought in."

Once the kayaks were all in the water, they followed the coastline. Sam dipped and pulled as hard as he could. Left, right. Left, right. He felt like a robot, except for the ache in his arms.

At first the thunder had been in the distance, but now a thunderbolt cracked close enough, and loud enough, to shake the kayak.

The marina appeared up ahead – almost safe. Wind churned the water, and a powerboat roared by, its wake a wide wave that rolled towards him. Sam braced his feet against the footplate, ready to take the force of the water. Would it be enough?

"Paddle . . . The wave!" shouted Billy.

What was Sam supposed to do?

Now Taneal was shouting, too. "Paddle!"

The racing wave reached the back of the kayak, and in an instant it had flipped it right over, dumping Sam into the lake. Icy water filled his eyes, his ears, his nose, his mouth.

For a few seconds, he was under the water – then under the kayak. He kicked away, letting the life jacket lift him to the surface. Another smaller wave washed over him, but at least he could see the shore again.

He coughed and spluttered, gasping to get his breath. It was only fifty metres or so to dry land.

"I've got the kayak," shouted Billy, and for a moment Sam watched it rocking on the water. It would be easier to swim to shore than to climb back into it. So, once he was breathing easily again, he started out – left, right, left, right, his arms slicing the water like kayak paddles.

Then he remembered the camera. What about the picture of the creature? What about the other pictures he'd taken, to show Grandpa all the places he couldn't walk to see himself. Sam treaded water and turned his head to look back but there didn't seem to be anything floating on the surface. Had his waterproof bag sunk to the bottom of the lake when the kayak overturned?

FOUR

Back at the cabin, Sam was rubbed down with a towel and cuddled and coddled as if he'd fallen into the water in the middle of winter. Grandma stood watch over him as if she were the only thing that stood between him and another dunking.

"Are you sure you don't want more orange juice?" Grandma asked, putting her right hand over his forehead.

"I'm all right, Grandma. No fever," said Sam.

"The boy's . . . good," said Grandpa. "Go on and see . . . the music."

"Yes, go, Grandma. Grandpa and I will be fine." There was a folk musician performing at the resort café that afternoon and Dad had already left to talk to him before he started playing. More research for his latest book probably. "Besides, it never even rained with all that thunder and lightning, so it won't be muddy out there."

"Well," said Grandma, her determination weakening, "if I can't do anything for either of you, maybe I will go and listen."

A loud thump at the door announced Taneal's arrival. "Hi, everyone," she said, walking in without waiting for anyone to answer her knock.

Grandma headed out the door with a light jacket over her arm as Taneal settled in on the couch.

"Exciting day?" asked Grandpa.

"For sure!" said Taneal. "I've already walked all along the shore by the dock twice, Sam, looking for your waterproof bag with the camera. The paddle washed in, but it was bigger. Billy says to just keep looking because there was air in the bag, so it'll float like a life jacket and turn up somewhere."

Sam tossed away the fluffy pale blue blanket Grandma had made him wrap up in. He was an adventurer, not a baby, after all. Getting rolled out of the kayak had been a kind of adventure – when he got home, he'd tell Tyler and Justin all about it. "Thanks. We can look again tomorrow."

"So . . . what did . . . you shoot?" asked Grandpa.

"I've got some great ones, Grandpa. Billy told us all about the different plants on shore. He even knew one bird call from another. I took lots of pictures and some video clips. I sure hope we can find the camera so you can see."

"But," said Taneal, glancing from Sam to his grandpa, "the one we really need is one Sam took from the kayak. It was of a really big creature on the shore."

"Another bear?"

Sam decided he had to be honest with Grandpa. "The picture I got today was so far away, it probably won't show anything. But I'm pretty sure it wasn't a bear."

"Me, too," said Taneal. "It just disappeared, poof, like something had zapped it with a magic wand! Yesterday, whatever we saw seemed bigger than a bear, and the thing we saw today didn't move like a bear."

Grandpa pointed at the laptop beside him. "So, let's take . . . a look again . . . at yesterday's photo."

"See," said Taneal, moving her fingers across the screen when they had the image displayed. "Bears don't walk around on their back legs like that in the forest. Maybe if they're curious they do, but not all the time. Today that creature on shore was always standing up, more like a person, and there wasn't anything much around that would interest a bear."

Grandpa nodded. "That's what . . . I've read."

"This creature is very big," said Sam. "It's bigger than a bear, isn't it?"

"Kodiak bears are the biggest," said Taneal. "I read about one that was more than three metres tall standing on its hind legs and weighed 680 kilograms."

"That's enormous!"

"Sure is," said Grandpa, staring more closely at the image on the computer screen.

"But kodiaks live in Alaska, not here smack

in the middle of Saskatchewan," said Taneal. "Moushoom says here and further north we have brown bears and black bears and all colours in between – like cinnamon bears."

"Cinnamon bears sound like they'd be good to eat," murmured Sam, zooming in a little on the picture.

Grandpa smiled and nodded towards the kitchen cupboards. "There are some gummy bears . . . on the top shelf."

Taneal went to investigate, and came back with a whole bag full of multicoloured chewy bears. "I'll put them in a bowl, so we can all have some."

Carefully, Sam picked out six orange bears – his favourite flavour – from the white cereal bowl she set down beside the computer. "Mmm . . . these are good. Thanks, Grandpa."

"You're welcome," said Grandpa, picking out a few for himself.

"But how big are bears here?" asked Sam.

Taneal finished the last bear in her hand. "Moushoom talks about one, an old black bear, maybe twenty-five years old or so, that weighed

300 kilograms and stood as tall on its hind legs as a big man."

"Do you think the creature we saw was taller than that?" asked Sam. What would he do if he ever got close to an animal like that?

Taneal nodded. "I'm pretty sure."

Grandpa pulled his walker close and stood up. "Search the Internet," he said. "I'm going to . . . lie down . . . rest a bit."

Sam watched as Grandpa slowly swish-swished across the floor, his slippered feet shining the golden hardwood as they slid one behind the other. While they'd been looking at the pictures and talking about what the creature might be, he had almost forgotten there was anything wrong. It had been almost like the old days, before the stroke.

"Ready?" asked Taneal.

"Sure." The laptop had a wireless connection to the Internet, so all Sam had to do was open a browser window to begin exploring. "What'll we look for?"

"How about creatures bigger than bears?"

The keys felt good under Sam's fingers. It had

been a week since he'd played a computer game. Amazing that he hadn't missed it before now!

Taneal ran her finger down the screen as if that were one more way of sifting through the information. "Nothing," she said at last.

Sam clicked on the second page of results. "What's a wampa ice creature?"

"I don't know. Click it and let's find out."

The page loaded slowly. "Star Wars," Sam groaned.

"Let's try again."

"Here's one," said Sam. "An owlbear." He clicked the mouse on the Wikipedia entry.

"Another magical beast," read Taneal. "This one from some role-playing game."

"We need a new search term," complained Sam, after scrolling through the top fifty entries. "This one isn't working."

"For sure."

"So what do we know about the creature?" asked Sam. "We can put it all in a search query."

"Well, we found it in the forest."

Sam typed in "forest". "And the forest was in

Saskatchewan. Should we use that or Canada?"

"Maybe Canada, since the creature could move around."

So Sam typed in "Canada" next to "forest".

Taneal stood up and stretched. "It's getting dark in here. We should open the curtains or turn on the lights."

"The only other thing I can think of is that it's big – a big creature, so we'll put in those two words, too." Sam clicked the mouse when he had finished typing in "big creature".

"Hey, what about a Bigfoot!" yelled Taneal, as she stared at the name of the first site returned in the search. "I forgot about them."

"What's a Bigfoot?" asked Sam, clicking on the link.

"Sometimes it's called Bigfoot and sometimes Sasquatch," explained Taneal. "Our teachers always said they don't really exist – like the Loch Ness monster. They say they're just myths people want to believe in and sometimes people make up hoaxes with Bigfoot clues and signs and fake pictures to convince other people that they're real."

"I did *not* see a hoax!"

"Me neither," said Taneal. "Moushoom says there's a story about a creature like that called a Rugaru. Our teacher said the Lakota people call it the Big Man, or Elder Brother, and think it's a spirit being that appears to bring you a message. Others think the Big Man exists in another dimension, like you see on television programmes, only the Big Man is more powerful than people and can move at will between them."

"Oh," said Sam. He didn't know what to think. Had he seen the creature because it had a message for him? Did that mean that, even if he didn't keep looking for it, he'd see it again anyway? "What do you want to call it, Taneal? You seem to know all about it."

"Hurray, you admit it!" said Taneal, doing a little dance of triumph. "I like Sasquatch best, because that's the name we used when we studied it at school."

"Your school sounds much more interesting than mine," said Sam enviously. "The most exciting creatures I've studied at school were dinosaurs – and there's no chance of ever seeing one of them for real."

An hour passed while Sam and Taneal pored over the computer, visiting website after website that mentioned Bigfoot and Sasquatch sightings. There were lots of hazy photographs and descriptions that seemed to match what they'd seen. But, instead of feeling he was getting to the bottom of the mystery, Sam felt a little more nervous with each website.

The evidence all seemed to point one way, however, and when Grandpa got up from his nap and asked them what they'd found, Sam and Taneal both shouted "Sasquatch!" at the same time.

"Really?" he said. "Tell me."

Scrolling through one of the best websites, Sam showed Grandpa pictures of the Sasquatch and read him descriptions of some eyewitness accounts. "Here's a sighting in Ontario. It talks about tracks being found. Each footprint was thirty-five centimetres long. That's enormous!"

"The creature has been sighted there off and on for more than twenty years," added Taneal. "They say that it looks like a man, but it's hairy all over."

"They guess the creature is very heavy, since its footsteps sink deep into the ground."

Grandpa nodded.

"I'm going to get a picture of it, Grandpa," said Sam, squeezing Grandpa's weathered hand in his – his hands weren't a lot bigger than Sam's these days. "A really good, clear picture that will prove it exists. Then we'll have a photograph that'll make us famous."

A tired smile crossed Grandpa's face, but all he said was, "Then you'll need . . . another camera. Yours . . . gone."

"We may find Sam's camera tomorrow, safe in its waterproof bag," said Taneal hopefully.

"Top shelf . . . " Grandpa pointed towards the open door of the bedroom, and the wardrobe beyond. He gestured for Sam to go and get whatever it was he wanted.

Sam couldn't reach the top shelf, so he called

for Taneal to bring him a chair and began digging around among the bags and surplus hats. "This, Grandpa?" he called, waving a red cloth bag that felt nearly empty.

"No."

Sam reached deeper. This time he pulled out a black, solid-sided bag and held it out where Grandpa could see it.

"That's it," said Grandpa. "Bring it . . . here."

"What is it?" asked Taneal.

Sam couldn't answer – he was too full of sadness and excitement all rolled up together. The bag held Grandpa's back-up camera – the camera he'd used to take his picture of the lion at the zoo. Everyone had told him it was so good he should enter it in some contests, but he'd just put it on the holiday calendar they'd made every year for their friends.

He handed the bag to Grandpa and he undid the zipper, pulled out the camera and put it in Sam's hands. "Sam, you've . . . earned it."

Sam felt a rush of joy mixed with worry. Did Grandpa really think he could use such a complicated camera? "But how will I know what buttons to push and settings to use? I can't do all that without you to show me."

"You'll figure . . . it out," said Grandpa. "You've been . . . helping me . . . take pictures with it . . . for four years already."

Taneal whistled long and low. "It's a beauty!" she said, as she watched Sam turn it on.

"First thing you need . . . is zoom," said Grandpa. He unpacked the extra lenses from the bag and ran his fingers over them. "You probably won't . . . see the animal . . . again. But . . . whatever animals you see . . . I want you . . . keep far back . . . safe."

Sam wondered how far back he'd have to be in order to be safe from a Sasquatch.

FIVE

Out on the lake shore, Sam crouched by the water with Grandpa's back-up camera, extra lens in place, around his neck and the gear bag strapped around his waist. He could remember when his job had been to carry it and dig out the lenses and filters whenever Grandpa asked for them.

"There's something there," whispered Taneal, pointing into the bulrushes.

Sam shook his head. "I don't see anything. Hey, there goes a frog again!" He bent down on one knee to aim the camera.

"If you're quiet, maybe it'll hop your way when I walk into the grass and bulrushes," said Taneal, slipping out of her shoes again. She splashed into the water.

The strong smell of still water and stirred-up mud and algae drifted back to Sam. So far, most of the bank they'd walked along had been covered with trees right to the water, or else tall grass. But in this part of the lake shore, the shallow water went out for a long way and seemed to be home to more creatures.

A frog croaked and hopped into camera range. Sam clicked the camera button and the picture appeared immediately on the display screen. This camera was much faster than his little one and easier to focus. If he ever saw the Sasquatch again, he would be able to get a really good shot.

He snapped another two pictures for luck, then pushed the review button to see them all – he even zoomed in on the last one to see if it was clear close up. It was.

"No sign of the bag," said Taneal, wading back.

"We should probably just give up looking for it," said Sam. "Maybe I didn't have the bag properly sealed and it filled up with lake water, and sank."

"No way! I want to see that shore picture and you've got all the other ones of the different plants that you wanted to show your grandpa." Taneal slipped her feet back into her shoes.

"Okay. We'll go as far as that bend up there and then stop."

Sam trudged further along the bank, keeping in the shade. It was the hottest day since he'd been here and the radio's breakfast announcer had said that it was going to reach thirty-five degrees today. It felt like it was almost that already.

A butterfly, its orange and black wings spread, fluttered past Sam's nose.

"A monarch!" gasped Taneal. "Moushoom says they never came this far north when he was small. He says they started just for me."

Sam grinned and turned the camera to follow the monarch's wavering flight. Click. A quick glance told him the image was blurry.

The butterfly hovered over a branch and landed.

Zoom. Click again.

This time the picture was almost perfect, just a little bit of one wing missing.

"That one's huge – at least ten centimetres," whispered Taneal. "It must have found some milkweed plants nearby for nectar."

"Have you ever seen monarchs that are greyish white instead of orange?" asked Sam. Maybe, just this once, he knew something about nature that Taneal didn't. He'd learned all about white monarchs when Grandpa had photographed one and they'd looked it up to find out what kind of butterfly it was, before adding the picture to their collection. He'd let Tyler use a copy of the picture in his science project on butterflies last winter, and the teacher had been very impressed.

Taneal shook her head. "Never."

Sam clicked again. "Grandpa and I got a picture of one two years ago. They're very rare – only one per cent of monarchs are that colour. I'll show you on his laptop when we get back."

Once he'd checked the photograph, they set off again. "Ouch," said Sam, swatting at a mosquito that landed on his hand. The repellent must be wearing off; it was definitely time to head back to the cabins.

"There!" shouted Taneal suddenly. "That's it!" And she raced off through the grass towards a metre-long piece of driftwood washed up on the bank.

Sure enough, there, snagged on one ragged end of the driftwood, puffed out like a small yellow pillow, was the missing plastic bag.

Sam ran, too, at the sight of it, but Taneal easily beat him to it. "Looks all right," she said, holding it up to show him.

"Don't open it yet," said Sam, though he desperately wanted to see if the camera still worked. "Let's just take it back and make sure the bag is all dried off before we look inside."

As they started the long walk back, an excited feeling began to build in Sam's chest, as if he were waiting in a long line for a roller coaster ride. His stomach even rolled. Would the camera still work? And would there be a picture of a Sasquatch?

"Sam!" Taneal poked him hard in the ribs. "Keep walking, but look over there – about ten metres into the trees."

"What . . . " Sam's words stopped at the same

time as his feet.

Just ahead to their right, a brown bear had lifted its head and was staring right at them. If they'd been closer, Sam could have leaned forward and rubbed its nose with his – the bear's nose was, however, a good deal larger than his was!

Taneal pushed him hard and said, even louder than before, "I told you not to stop. Bears don't like to be surprised. Keep walking and talking."

Sam heard her words, but they seemed to blow up and away, like a kite suddenly free of its string on a windy day.

The bear shifted, rose up on its hind legs and sniffed the air.

Did he dare turn on his camera to get a picture? Not yet. Sam found his voice. "Bears look scary close up."

"This one's just young, probably only born a couple of years ago," said Taneal, still speaking loudly. "Wait until you see a big, grouchy mama bear!" She stomped hard on some fallen branches so that they snapped and crackled.

Stomp. Crunch. Crack. Stomp. Sam began to

move again, taking small steps, his finger pushed down on the camera's power switch.

"Don't slow down," warned Taneal.

"I'm not! I thought I could just turn the camera to the movie setting and point it." He didn't dare take his eyes off the bear to look at the camera.

The bear dropped to all fours. "Woof, woof," it rumbled, almost like a dog, though its voice was much deeper and scarier.

In another few steps they'd be almost even with the bear – safety was a lot further away!

"Why did it drop to the ground like that?" asked Sam. Was it getting ready to attack them? Did Taneal really know what to do? Should he do what she said, or should he take to his heels and run as fast as he could away from here?

"The bear probably just thinks we're after its berries, so keep walking!"

The bear's head moved to follow their progress. It opened its mouth and a long, slow growl filled the space between them and it.

"Now we worry!" said Taneal. "Walk a little faster, but don't run!"

Another growl – shorter and louder this time.

A jolt of terror ran right through Sam, from his toenails up to his eyelashes.

"Don't look it in the eye," ordered Taneal, "or it'll be sure that you're challenging it."

How was Sam supposed to make sure he didn't look the bear in the eye and still keep watching it? He leaned to his left and reached out his hand to grab a metre-long dried branch.

"No!" shouted Taneal, grabbing his arm and jerking him back onto the path they'd tramped along earlier without a care in the world. "What would you think if somebody grabbed a stick when they were this close to you?"

Sam's heart raced as fast as the motorbikes on his favourite video game. He felt sure the bear would be able to hear it. "That they might be going to hit me with it, I guess . . . "

"That's what the bear will think, too!"

"What," asked Sam slowly, "would it do, do you think, if it thought it had to protect itself . . . from us . . . right now?"

"Roar and chase us," snapped Taneal. "Just like you would!"

The bear remained on all fours, watching every step they took, gathered ready to charge.

Left, right. Left, right. Crunch. Thump. Thud. Sam concentrated on the sound of his footsteps as he walked past the bear, each step now taking him further away.

At last, the bear shifted its gaze away from them and turned back towards the trees. Standing upright, it pulled a low branch of a shrub towards it and began plucking the berries with its mouth.

"It's eating," said Sam, still walking, his head turned awkwardly to watch. "Does that mean it's decided we're not a threat?"

"I think so. It'll forget all about us now that it's busy."

In the bear's place, thought Sam, he wouldn't be forgetting so easily! "What kind of berries is it eating?"

"Raspberries. Like these," said Taneal. Calmly, she walked another ten metres along the path, stepped into the bush and brought back a branch laden with bright red berries. After picking a few and popping them into her mouth, she held it out towards him. "Have some."

"Is it safe to stop yet?" mumbled Sam, ignoring the offered branch. The wild thumping of his heart had slowed, but he now felt as tired as if he'd just run a couple of kilometres.

"Sure," said Taneal, turning back to the berries.

Sam glanced at the camera. It was still on. How could he have been foolish enough to think he could get pictures of wild animals so easily?

"Is it really safe to stop?" he repeated numbly.

Taneal nodded. "The wind is blowing our scent away from it now. It'll think we've gone."

By the time Sam turned back to look, all he could see was trees. The bear had disappeared.

"We're back, Grandma," called Sam as he opened the cabin door.

Nobody answered.

Sam walked around the large front room that combined kitchen, dining room and living room, then looked through the open bedroom door. Nobody. The bathroom door was open, too – and also empty.

"Maybe they all went for coffee?" suggested Taneal, peering over his shoulder. "The office lady said that Shelley, the waitress at the restaurant, picked two buckets of strawberries yesterday and the cook was going to make rhubarb and strawberry pies this morning."

How did Taneal always know all about whatever was going on?

"Sounds good," muttered Sam, wishing his family had waited so he could have gone along, too. "I wonder if drying the bag with a towel will be enough?"

"Maybe your grandma has a hair dryer." Taneal marched into the bathroom and gazed around. "Here! It's all plugged in and ready to go."

Sam handed her the bag, which was now no more than a little damp after their long, hot hike, and Taneal blew hot air all over the sides, bottom and rolled-down top. "Do you want to open it?" she asked, holding the bag out to him.

For a second, Sam just looked at it. A beach ball seemed to bounce its way through his stomach and catch in his throat, taking his breath away. It didn't look as if there was any steam or drops of water on the inside of the bag. Surely the camera would be all right.

"I guess," said Sam.

Taneal put the bag in his hand.

Slowly, he reached deep inside it and pulled out its contents. The brown paper lunch bag. Dry. The plastic sandwich container. Dry. The granola bar wrapper. Dry. And, finally, the camera. Dry, too!

When he pushed the on button, the camera came to life with its usual little ring tone. Hurray, it was working!

Sam connected the camera to Grandpa's laptop and sat down on the couch to wait for the images to download.

"What are you going to do if you get a picture that proves the Sasquatch is real?" asked Taneal, then answered herself. "Get it in some newspapers, I suppose. Put it on the Internet for sure, so everybody hears about it. I'll bet your grandpa would be proud."

For some reason, the idea didn't delight Sam the way he would have expected. Instead, he found himself talking about Grandpa. "He's been a photographer his whole life, taking pictures of families and new babies. But summer holidays, he says, are for doing what you love, not what you have to do, so we've been taking nature pictures every year since I could hardly carry the gear bag. The only other time we see each other is a few days at Christmas."

After meeting the bear, the thought of getting close to an even bigger Sasquatch filled Sam with dread. Maybe he should stick to taking pictures of butterflies and frogs?

SIX

Later, when Taneal had gone and Grandma and Grandpa returned, Sam told them about seeing the young bear. But he didn't say how close they had been to it – or that it was too dangerous even to try to get a picture.

A flash of lightning brightened the inside of the cabin as they talked. "Heat like this always brings on a storm," said Grandpa. He unplugged the laptop and let it run on its battery.

Staring at the photo on the laptop screen, Sam realised that the glare from the sun reflecting on the water while he was taking it had made everything dark. The picture didn't look like much of anything – just a stretch of water and a shadowy distant shape that blurred into the darker trees. No Sasquatch.

"Sun messes up . . . exposure time," said Grandpa, changing screens on the computer and bringing up a file of photos labelled "exposure". He clicked on a picture of a howler monkey, hanging from a tree branch.

"I remember that picture!" said Sam. It was taken during their holiday two years ago, when they'd walked around the monkey cage at the zoo, snapping shots from different angles. "This is the one that took the longest because we had to wait for the monkey to swing by one arm, so it would make a silhouette. In the first pictures of just the monkey sitting in the tree, we couldn't tell where the tree ended and the monkey began."

Grandpa nodded and smiled, as if he were pleased that Sam had immediately seen what he was trying to show him. "No detail . . . without different exposure time . . . or a filter." He pointed at the camera bag he'd given Sam yesterday.

Sam handed it to him and together they looked through the filters that went over the lens, until Grandpa picked one and held it out. "This one."

Along the side were the words "neutral density filter". Sam didn't understand what that meant, but he could remember how often he had found this particular attachment for Grandpa. "If I'd had this filter on, we could have seen what was on shore instead of dark blobs, right?"

"Yes." Grandpa took the big camera and clicked on the menu as Sam peered over his shoulder. "Or you could change . . . exposure."

Thump, thump, thump. As usual, Taneal burst in without waiting for anyone to open the door for her.

"Whew. It's wet!" Rainwater ran off the large black plastic garbage bag she was holding like an umbrella over her head and shoulders for protection.

Through the open door behind her, Sam could see a dark curtain of rain lit up by lightning zigzagging across the sky, followed a few seconds later by a crack of thunder.

Grandma came out of the bedroom and hurried to the door with a towel and a mop from the bathroom. "Goodness, it's certainly coming down. Are you wet, dear?"

"Not really," replied Taneal, though she took the towel Grandma offered and ran it quickly over her hair and face. She stepped out of her sodden shoes, took a step, then realised she needed to dry her feet, too. They had left neat wet footprints behind her on the wooden floor.

"It's all right, dear," said Grandma. She ran the mop over the floor by the door. "I'm so glad you were with Sam this morning when he saw that bear. You're such a clever girl."

Taneal towelled her feet. "I just do what my moushoom taught me."

"Well," said Grandma, giving her a hug, "then I'm glad you're such a good learner."

Boom! This time the crack of thunder went on for three long, loud seconds. As the sound rolled to an end, the lights blinked and went out. It was just past three in the afternoon, but the room grew dark without them.

"The lightning must've hit somewhere," said Grandma. "No power for a while, I imagine."

"Good thing Dad's got extra batteries for his laptop," said Taneal. "He's working on the creature profiles for the game today. He wants to finish by the weekend."

Yes! Sam punched the air. If Taneal's dad finished developing the game soon, maybe Sam would be able to give it a trial run!

"Well, I'm sure we can find something for you two to do this afternoon that doesn't need any power," said Grandma.

"Chequers," said Grandpa. That was always Grandpa's first choice. Before the stroke, he'd been the chequers champion of the whole family. Sam wondered if he'd still be able to play or whether that had been lost, too, like his words and his ability to walk freely.

While Grandma went back into the bedroom for the games box, Taneal flopped down on the couch in front of the laptop.

"Could you fix the picture?" she asked.

"Not really. We tried adjusting it, but you still can't see much of anything."

"Oh well," she sighed. "Maybe tomorrow."

For the rest of that afternoon, they had a chequers tournament. Sam and Taneal played the first game, followed by Grandpa and Grandma. Then the winners and losers played each other, followed by more rounds of winners against winners and losers against losers.

"This is it, the final game," declared Grandma. "I'm too old for all this excitement."

Taneal checked her watch. "Dad said I had to be home by six."

"Ready?" asked Grandpa, settling the last red chequer in the right square.

"Ready," said Taneal, straightening her shoulders and taking a deep breath. "Be prepared to lose, Mr Christos!"

"You go, girl!" cheered Grandma, waving a pink silk scarf she'd tied on to a pair of chopsticks as a flag.

Sam held up his own flag – which consisted of Grandpa's lion photo T-shirt draped over a rolling pin, tied on with rubber bands – and cheered, "Go, Grandpa, go! Go, Grandpa, go!"

Sam was so intent on the game, he didn't even hear Dad open the cabin door when he came home from another day of research at the Prince Albert Library.

"Hey," shouted Dad, making Sam jump. "Can I join in?"

"You can cheer," said Grandma, pulling the armchair closer for him to sit in. "You're too late for the tournament."

"I guess that'll have to do." Dad added his shoes to the long row at the door and sat down between Sam and Grandma.

"Your move," said Grandpa to Taneal.

Taneal stared at the board, thought for a minute, then slid a black chequer horizontally.

Grandma waved her flag and chanted, "Girls, girls, girls, we're in the groove. Watch us win, we got the moves!"

Dad laughed. "I guess I'd better join the boys' cheering squad. How about, 'Here's to Grandpa, he's true blue, he's a champion through and through!'"

"Pretty old cheer," said Grandpa, without looking up from the board, but he was smiling.

It only took him another three moves to defeat Taneal and, when he did, everyone cheered, even Taneal. "Hurray for Grandpa!"

Later that night, Sam lay in bed, listening to the song of the loons and thinking that, if he could get a picture of the Sasquatch, this holiday would be perfect after all.

When sunshine began to fill the cabin the next morning, he looked out to see a broken film of water surrounding it, like a moat in the days of old King Arthur.

"Hi, everybody," said Taneal, bursting into the cabin in a pair of red rubber boots that came nearly up to her knees. She was carrying a second pair of black ones.

"Good morning, Taneal," said Grandma. "Well, you look ready for the day."

Sam gulped down his last spoonful of oatmeal and brown sugar. "Can we go out taking pictures, Dad?"

Dad lifted his head from the newspaper, just as he did every morning at home when Mum left for the office. "I don't see why not."

Taneal held out the black boots. "I borrowed these for you. They belong to the office lady's daughter's friend's kid."

"Thanks." Sam wondered how Taneal

managed to keep track of so many little details all the time. He put a foot in one of the boots and wiggled his toes. It was only a little too big.

"Forgetting something?" asked Taneal.

"Don't worry, I'm getting to it," said Sam, stepping out of the boots to gather up everything he needed for the day. "I thought you might want to use the little digital camera, Taneal." He held it out to her as he put Grandpa's old one around his neck and fastened the camera waist bag.

"Wow! Me a photographer?" She looped the strap around her neck.

"So you're set then." Grandpa had a faraway look in his eyes, as if he were thinking of something else.

"No more wandering so far out along the lake shore," said Dad. "Keep to the paths. I know Taneal's dad says there's never been a bear attack around here, but that may just be because everyone is being very careful."

"I'm older than Sam," said Taneal, "so he has to listen to me. I won't let him get into trouble."

Grandma smiled. "I'm sure you won't. But today I want you to take my cellphone with you, just in case." She handed it to Sam.

"Grandma, we'll be all right," he said.

"Maybe, but I want to be able to talk to you whenever I want, and to know for myself that you're fine."

"Okay." Sam added the cellphone to his camera bag and pulled the cabin door open. "See you later, everybody."

Taneal followed him out, splashing through the puddles in her big red boots. The water was everywhere. At the foot of the cabin steps. In the middle of the road. Under the trees.

"Where do you want to go?" asked Taneal, joining Sam by a tall pine with her bike.

"I think we should go back to where I took that first picture – the one with you in it. That was on a path."

"All right. Can you show me how to take a picture before we get there? You know, so I can be ready in case we see the creature this morning."

"It's easy. You just push the on button at the top first," said Sam, demonstrating. Musical notes sounded as the camera came to life.

"Now hold the camera up and look through the square screen on the back. That's the viewfinder."

"I feel like a movie producer, deciding what to film," said Taneal, backing up a few steps. "Now how do I take a picture of you, Sam?"

"That silver button on top – it's on the right side – you just hold it down a little to focus the picture, then push it all the way down to snap it. Or you can just push it all the way at once, but then sometimes it's not focused."

Click! They gathered around the tiny screen to look at Taneal's first picture – she had cut half his head off.

"Not too bad," said Sam kindly – then he showed her how to play all the images back.

"This is how you delete them, if you want." Sam selected the option from the menu. "Click 'yes' and it's gone."

Snap! Snap! Snap! Taneal took the camera back and clicked off picture after picture as Sam jumped on his bike and rode through the centre of a puddle. Muddy water hit his face, his arms, his legs.

"Hey, you're camouflaged!" shouted Taneal excitedly. "We could ride right by a bear without it seeing us."

Some of the pictures turned out well. Some weren't bad. And some were plain awful. But Taneal remained unconcerned. "I like taking pictures. Maybe I'll be a photographer like you and your grandpa."

She picked up her bike and pedalled straight into a puddle, sinking deep into the mud.

They were laughing so hard as they rode away, their bikes wobbled and lurched all over the path.

"Hey, Sam, isn't this the spot where you first saw the Sasquatch?"

Sam nodded. Would they find the creature today? After yesterday's chance meeting with the bear, he hoped it wouldn't be too close if they did find it. Especially now that he had a good zoom camera.

It felt good to walk in the shade of the tall

evergreens. Pedalling through the mud had been hard work. Sam peered through the trees, trying to find some sign of the creature.

A raven cawed. A squirrel scurried around a tree, anxious to get out of the way. Sam snapped a picture of it running and only caught its tail.

"Nothing," said Taneal, her shoulders slumped with disappointment.

Suddenly, the cellphone in Sam's waist bag started ringing – a loud, alien sound in the quiet woodland. He pulled it out and flipped it open. "Hello, Grandma . . . Yes, we're on a path . . . Everything's fine . . . Bye."

"My moushoom worries sometimes, too," said Taneal. "He tells me that it's because he loves me."

Sam nodded. "Anyway, let's follow the mountain bike and quad bike trails further. Maybe we'll see some animals and we can practise taking pictures."

"This way," said Taneal, following a path to the right.

Fifty or so pictures later, Sam and Taneal reached a steeper area where erosion had eaten away at the earth and grass cover.

"Guess we might as well go back. I'm getting hungry," said Sam.

"All right."

Sam held up the camera and zoomed in for one last picture. All he could see was clumps of grass, lumps of crumbling soil and huge, muddy footprints. *Muddy footprints?* What could make footprints as long as that?

The Sasquatch! It had been here!

"Taneal, look!" shouted Sam, running through the grass to get as near as he could to the tracks. "The Sasquatch has been here and left enormous footprints behind, just like on the Internet. Let's get some pictures!"

SEVEN

Sam stared at the picture of footprints on the laptop monitor. "But, Grandpa, they're enormous. They really are."

"This big at least, Mrs Christos," added Taneal, stretching her arms apart to show Grandma just how huge they had been.

Grandpa smiled. Grandma smiled. Dad smiled.

"Maybe it was that bear sliding around on the slippery mud," suggested Grandma. "I'm just glad you didn't see it again."

Dad took one last look, then went back to the pile of notes and photocopied papers he had laid out on the kitchen table. "When there are fewer trees, as in this area, and it's steeper, the ground wears away more easily. Somebody else must have stopped there before you. Maybe another bear."

Grandma picked up the basket of clothes she'd dropped in the armchair. "I'm going to get the washing out of the way this morning, so I'll be over at the resort laundry if you need me."

Sam stared at Grandpa. Surely, if he examined the photograph more closely, Grandpa would know it wasn't somebody's stray footprint or a bear.

"Let's take a . . . better look," said Grandpa.

"All right!" Sam dropped down on the floor beside Grandpa and Taneal went around the other side of the couch and balanced on the thick padded arm. "It was so big, Mr Christos! I never saw anything like it before."

"First," said Grandpa, "we'll zoom in." In a second, the whole computer screen was filled with muddy brown indentations that looked like tiny hills and valleys.

Sam took off his sock and ran his fingers over the ball of his foot, past his toes, through the centre where Mum liked to tickle his feet. It was likely his muddy footprint would appear similar to the one they'd found.

"That's too much magnification," muttered Grandpa. He zoomed back out a bit, so the single clearest print was centred on the screen.

"It's not a bear," said Taneal. "I know it and I can prove it. We just need to find some bear tracks on the Internet to compare it with."

Sam nodded. "Good idea!"

Grandpa changed windows and brought up the search engine.

"Try that one," said Taneal, touching the screen as a page of possible images to choose from appeared.

The bear track was long and narrow, with all five toes pointing out at the top.

"That looks just about like my foot," said Sam, "except my toenails aren't so long."

"Claws," said Grandpa. "They can't pull 'em back."

Taneal nodded. "Moushoom says the bears need claws for protection and climbing trees. In the long ago time, bear claws represented healing, so a man was lucky to possess them."

"Can you change screens, Grandpa?"

Click-click. Sam and Taneal and Grandpa all stared at this morning's photograph. It didn't have any claw marks.

"Let's look some more," said Grandpa, switching back to the photos of bear tracks.

Click-click. That photo only showed the front of a foot.

Click-click. That photo showed a foot that was fat at the front where the toes were and skinny at the back where the heel was.

Click-click. That photo looked a lot like the photo they'd taken this morning – it didn't even have claw tracks at the top.

"But I'm sure it's not a bear," said Taneal. She sat back and took a deep breath. "For sure, it's bigger than a bear's foot."

Dad glanced up from his papers. "Different kinds of bears have different-sized feet, just like people. Perhaps this is a bear of a species that isn't usually around here, Taneal."

"Well . . . Moushoom says many strange things are happening in the north with climate change. I suppose . . . "

Sam wasn't ready to give up yet. "Let's go

back and measure the biggest whole footprint. I'll bet it's way longer than a bear's."

"Good idea," said Grandpa. "You need a . . . measuring tape."

"Sorry, nothing like that here," said Dad with a smile. "We didn't pack for Sasquatch hunting expeditions. Perhaps someone in the resort office can lend you something?"

The muddy road was already starting to dry up in the breeze and the heat by the time they started pedalling back to the muddy tracks. It had only taken Sam a few minutes to borrow what they needed, say goodbye to Grandma at the laundry and assure her the cellphone was still working.

"It sure is hot," said Sam, letting the bike coast for a moment as he caught his breath.

"It always is after a big rain," replied Taneal. "This is the best kind of day for a dip in the lake – the cold water really feels good!"

"Maybe Dad or Grandpa would come down

to the beach this afternoon so we could go in the water," suggested Sam.

"Dad's just testing the game next week, so he'll have some time." Taneal pulled her bike to the side as two boys riding quad bikes roared down the road towards them. "Moushoom has a quad bike now for hauling our things into the bush when we go camping. It sure is better than carrying them."

Sam watched the machines for a moment as they passed. "I still like bicycles better."

The path to the mysterious tracks seemed a lot longer than it had when the weather was cooler. Sam stopped to rest and taste a few sweet raspberries from a bush. Taneal rested in the shade while he tried to whistle the same fee-bee, fee-bee song as a flycatcher high in the trees. He caught a whiff of the stink of a skunk and scanned the path and trees, hoping they wouldn't see it, even at a distance.

Finally, they reached the spot, but it had changed since they'd last seen it.

"Oh no!" said Sam, shaking his head in disbelief.

"Those quad bikes have been here," fumed Taneal. "They've driven all over everything!"

Fat tyre tracks now crisscrossed the whole area. Some went left. Some went right. Some spun around in swishy circles. Little piles of mud, like animal droppings, surrounded the gouges made by spinning tyres.

The longer Sam stared at the mess, the angrier he got. "Couldn't they see there were strange tracks here?" How were they going to measure the footprints and prove it was a Sasquatch, not a bear?

"What do they care!" said Taneal. "They're probably out looking for some other place to rip up for fun."

"Why would they do that?"

"My dad says some people don't understand how much damage they're doing to the parks when they get off the trails and tear up the land, but I think they're like bullies and they just do it to be mean because some of us want to protect the environment."

Sam thought about that for a while. "Last year at school, bullies took this little kid's brand new backpack and drove over it with their bikes. I got so mad I started yelling and throwing stones at them to make them stop. The teacher on playground duty made us all go to the office and I got a suspension, just like them. My dad took away my video games for a whole month."

"That wasn't fair!"

"I shouldn't have thrown the rocks, I guess, but there were three of them and only one of me, plus the little kid of course. My mum said I should have just gone for the playground teacher in the first place."

"Yeah, that's what my dad would say, too." Taneal grinned. "Wonder what they'd do if they were actually there?"

"Me, too." Sam laid his bike down in the grass and surveyed the destruction. "Let's just try to find the clearest track we can and measure it." He dug in his camera waist bag for the bright orange measuring tape they'd borrowed.

"Yeah. No sense in giving up before we have to," said Taneal.

Together they walked in a wide circle around the quad tracks, keeping to the grassy edges that had only been partly torn up.

Sam stopped and pointed at the ground. "That was the biggest one, wasn't it?"

Except for the longest, the toe marks on the footprint were almost gone now, replaced with tyre tread. In the middle, the print had been stretched, as if it were pie dough under a rolling pin. A few mud lumps were clumped together where the heel should have been.

"It was the best one," agreed Taneal. "I guess we'd better take more pictures before we measure it. Too bad we'll only be able to show your grandpa what it looks like now."

Back at the cabin, Sam and Taneal stood on either side of the laptop as Grandpa shook his head in dismay over the images. "Too bad . . . It's too bad."

"We're pretty sure the footprint was fifty centimetres long, even with all that driving over it," said Sam, staring anxiously at Grandpa.

"That's way longer than a bear's print," added

Taneal. "At least, I'm pretty sure it is."

"Let's look it up on the Internet."

Grandpa changed screens again and they began the search for more information about bear tracks. One site. Three sites. Five sites. They tried new search terms, but still couldn't find exact measurements for the size of a bear's foot.

Finally, they tried a Natural History Museum site that had lots of information about the tracks of black bears.

"That's the kind that are here, isn't it?" asked Sam, as they all peered at the screen, trying to find the information they wanted.

"Yup," said Taneal. "Hey, here it is! The site says they're fourteen inches long. How many centimetres is that?"

"Around thirty-five," said Grandpa, turning to face them. "That's no black bear . . . out there. Maybe it's a much bigger bear . . . come down from the far north. Or it isn't a bear."

"We're right!" shouted Sam. He cheered.

Taneal cheered, too.

But, when Sam saw the looks on Grandpa

and Dad's faces, his cheers died.

Now Grandpa and Dad were exchanging glances.

"No more creature hunting," said Grandpa after a moment.

"And no investigating those tracks either," said Dad, even more firmly.

EIGHT

Sam was bored. He'd already taken photographs of absolutely everything around the cabins in Anglin Lake village, and the playground, and the boat ramp, and the office and café at Land of the Loon. Grandpa had beaten him three times at chequers and he'd beaten Grandpa three times. It was a draw. He'd helped Grandma make chocolate chip cookies and then eaten half of them.

Taneal sat at the table with his dad, working on a story about the Sasquatch, and having lots of fun. It seemed to Sam that she must write the way she talked – hundreds and hundreds of words at a mad gallop. Would she ever stop?

"Sam," said Grandma, "would you like to come with me to Waskesiu to do a little shopping? How about you, Taneal?"

"I'm still writing," answered Taneal, without even lifting her head.

Sam sighed. "Guess I'll come with you, Grandma."

Dad seemed happy to have somebody with him who enjoyed writing as much as he did. "I'm sure Taneal and I will still be writing when you get back."

So, while Grandma drove the rental car, Sam stared out the window, watching the trees go by. In a few more days, Mum would be here – and Taneal and her dad would probably be gone to visit her moushoom in the north.

He was never going to get a photograph of the Sasquatch.

The little town, when they reached it, seemed as busy as back home in the city. Waskesiu was the only village in Prince Albert National Park, the oldest national park in Saskatchewan.

When Sam's family had been researching where to go for this holiday, Grandpa had chosen it because the park contained different eco-zones. Between the parklands, prairie and forest, there were habitats for many different types of animals. He and Grandpa had planned to take at least a thousand pictures to add to their collection.

It was Mum and Grandma who had chosen Land of the Loon Resort, because the cabins were big enough for them all to share, but Sam would have chosen it for the name alone. And Dad was happy as long as he was close to the Prince Albert Library, where he'd planned to research a new novel.

Sam started thinking about what Taneal had said about the Big Man appearing to people it had a message for. If he and Grandpa had been out hiking every day as they had planned, would they have a clear picture of the Sasquatch by now? Or would they have seen it at all? What if there really was some reason nobody else in the Anglin Lake community had seen it?

Grandma pulled their rental car into the only empty space near the grocery store. "We'll stop here first."

An enormous motor-home roared down the narrow street behind them, almost touching the back of the parked cars. Two boys, both younger than Sam, barrelled down the footpath on skateboards. "Watch for traffic, boys," called a lady pushing a baby in a pushchair.

Across the street, three teenaged girls licked ice cream cones, giggling loudly and waving at a boy on a red quad bike. He wasn't one of the riders they'd seen this morning.

"Come on, Sam," said Grandma, stopping in the shop doorway. "I could do with your help."

It didn't take long for Grandma to fill up the small grocery trolley that Sam pushed. But it seemed to take forever to get to the front of the line-up at the cash register. While he waited, Sam listened to two elderly men talking. One picked up a tabloid newspaper from the stand and pointed out items of interest to the other.

"Just look here," he said, bending his bald head, suntanned a deep golden shade of brown, over the paper to read the words. "Crop circles again. Sure am glad I'm not farmin' no more, not with these crazy news hounds runnin' around takin' pictures."

"No good ever comes out of a news panic,"

said the second, his voice raspy and loud.

"They're not lookin' for news! These young hot shots are lookin' for a *story* about some fool who'd go out in a field and tromp the grain down in shapes that look like circles, tryin' to make everybody think it might be alien spaceships."

The raspy-voiced man nodded. "They don't find a story, they go ahead and make one up. Aliens or hoaxers, they don't care which, long as it sells papers."

"Back in '90, when my neighbour found crop circles in his field, I near enough couldn't finish up my own harvest for all the crazies drivin' around in my fields. Looky-lous were stragglin' in for a year after, makin' a mess and wreckin' things."

The newspaper rustled as the other man turned the page, "It sure don't . . . "

"Sam, help me with these bags." Grandma's voice drowned out whatever the men had to say next. "I think we'll make a quick stop at the bakery, too."

Sam wished he could have heard more of the men's conversation – it sounded interesting.

Whatever, it couldn't hurt to find out more about crop circles.

Back at Land of the Loon, Taneal had been called home by her dad, and she was already gone. Sam helped Grandma unpack the bags and put everything away, then headed straight for the laptop, while Grandpa lay down for a rest before dinner.

Sure enough, he found lots of articles about crop circles near here in 1990. It sounded like newspapers from all over the country had covered the story. And nobody ever found out for sure who made the circles or why.

He also found a story about another Sam who'd seen a creature he called Bigfoot. People had come from all over for years and years and years, trying to track it or find proof that it existed. The same thing had happened in Colorado and British Columbia and Virginia. As soon as someone thought they'd found the creature, hundreds of others showed up to get their own story and pictures. Some of the articles said the only real proof scientists would accept these days was a real live Sasquatch that they could study and keep like a zoo animal.

Sam felt a renewed surge of excitement. He needed to get such good photographs that people around the world would just have to believe that the Sasquatch was real.

Grandma's pasta sauce tasted as good as it always did at dinner, and when everyone had finished he gathered up the dishes, washed them and settled in a patio chair to read. But each time he heard a bird hoot, a voice call or a bike chain rattle, he dropped the book, sure it must be Taneal. Surely, she'd come over tonight. She had left without saying goodbye.

Finally, she appeared. "Hi, everyone," she called, as she leaned her bike against the deck. "My dad says we can go for a short bike ride tonight. That's if you can, Sam."

Sam marked his page with a bookmark and thought about how to get everyone to agree that he could go out for a while. The encounter with the bear and the saga of the Sasquatch tracks seemed to be making them edgy and anxious. Who knew how they'd react to a nocturnal bike ride. He glanced at Grandpa, sitting with the camera beside him on the table. If he was fit, he'd have been out every day and every evening, taking pictures of birds and sunsets. Yes, that was it! Sam could get some photos of sunset over Anglin Lake for Grandpa.

"Can I go down to the lake, Dad? Please? Grandpa, we need sunset pictures of Anglin Lake, don't we?"

Dad glanced from Grandpa to Sam and then to Taneal. "Where exactly do you want to go, Taneal?"

"Just down past the boat ramp," she said, glancing at Sam. "Dad made me promise not to go looking for the Sasquatch."

"Grandpa, please!"

"It's up to your dad, Sam," said Grandpa. "If I could, I'd go. I imagine the lake is beautiful this last hour before sunset. But I can't . . . " His words trailed off as his gaze came to rest on his walker.

"I'd go with you," said Dad, "but I'm meeting

one of the locals for coffee. I have to ask him some questions for my next book. So it looks as if I'm going to have to trust you, Sam. Do you promise to stay within sight of the boat ramp?"

"I promise!" shouted Sam and Taneal at the same time.

"Well . . . all right."

"Thanks, Dad!" said Sam. "Grandpa, I'm going to get the best sunset pictures ever."

"You'd better put on long pants and a long-sleeved shirt, maybe some bug spray, too," said Taneal, grabbing the small camera. "The mosquitoes get especially thirsty at night."

"Just like vampires!"

When they were ready, Sam checked once more that everything was in the camera bag, then did the belt up around his waist.

"Goodbye, everyone," he called, doing a last ride-by the cabin steps on his bicycle.

"Get some good pictures!" Grandpa called back.

With the heat of the day long gone, Sam found it easy to pedal hard in the cool air, following Taneal on the shortcut through the trees and onto the road.

"Have you ever seen a crop circle?" he asked, remembering the conversation he'd overheard that afternoon.

Taneal shook her head. "Lots of people don't believe they're real. They say it's kids playing a joke. They go out and make marks in the fields just to fool people."

"I don't think that's very funny." Sam thought about the man who'd said people had tramped through his fields and kept coming around for a whole year, wrecking things.

When they reached the boat ramp, there was only one truck and trailer parked there, waiting for a boat to come in for the night.

"See there?" said Taneal, her voice dropping to a whisper. "Looks like something moving in the trees along the shore."

"A deer?" Sam whispered back. He could see a moving shape, too.

"Probably. They often come through there to

drink." She pointed further down the lake bank. "Let's go over by that big fallen tree."

A loon wailed – whooo-oooo – then another and another.

"They sound so sad," said Sam.

When they reached the fallen tree, Sam took the camera out of the bag and peered through the viewfinder. The fading light made the lake glisten and shimmer. It looked very different from the way it had in the daylight. He turned in a wide half-circle, snapping six or seven pictures.

Taneal settled down with her back against the fallen tree, and propped her chin on her knees to watch the lake. "See there? A pike jumping."

Sam hadn't seen the fish, but the ripples from where it had dived spread out over the glassy surface of the water. He snapped again.

A sound like crazy laughter echoed across the water as Sam switched off the camera and sat down next to Taneal. "What was that?"

"A loon. That's their alarm call. Something must be nearby, coming down for water."

"Got your camera ready?" asked Sam,

switching the camera on again and holding up the viewfinder. Zoom. A loon filled half the screen. If only he'd had this camera on the lake yesterday, he might already have a perfect picture of the Sasquatch.

And then he heard another sound.

It started like a baby's cry. Without stopping, the sound grew deeper, more like a dog's howl. And, finally, the pitch changed and became angry, then built into a squeal of anguish.

Sam's heart thudded and lurched, almost as if he'd run smack into whatever creature had made that noise. "What was that?" he whispered, once he could breathe again.

Taneal shook her head. "Not a loon . . . "

"A bear?"

Taneal shook her head again. "Never heard a bear wail like that!"

Sam and Taneal crouched down behind the fallen tree, hoping it would hide them from whatever was out there, looking vainly in the direction he guessed the sound had come from.

Was it an animal? wondered Sam. Should he try to take its picture? Would he be *able* to take its picture? His hands shook as he tried to steady the camera.

The horrifying sound came again, closer this time, as if the animal were moving.

And then there it was – the creature!

It was standing upright, tall and straight like a person and at least two and a half metres tall. Long, rag-doll arms hung from its broad shoulders and straggly, brownish hair covered its head, arms, body and legs – even its feet.

It was a Sasquatch!

NINE

The Sasquatch howled again, louder than the pack of coyotes Sam had heard at Land of the Loon, raising their voices on moonlit nights.

His hands shook so much, his finger wouldn't stay on top of the camera's power switch. The bear they'd seen yesterday had been only half as big as this Sasquatch – only half as dangerous.

What on earth were they going to do?

In all of the stories Sam had read, nobody had ever described being as close as this to a Sasquatch. In the videos, it seemed the people only had to point the camera at the creature and it ran away into the forest.

This Sasquatch didn't look as if it intended to run away. If he tried to take its picture it would probably grab the camera, crumple it up like a piece of used tissue and toss it away.

The Sasquatches he'd read about on the websites had all sounded friendly. Some had given people gifts. Some had even communicated with them. But this one didn't look the least bit friendly. With 400 sightings every year, surely somebody else had seen an unfriendly one. He wished they'd said what they did to survive.

"What should we do?" whispered Sam.

"I don't know," Taneal whispered back. "I never saw a Sasquatch before and neither has anybody I know."

Sam glanced at his camera, but didn't dare make a noise by pressing the button to take a picture. Perhaps the Sasquatch had keen hearing, like a lion that could detect its prey from more than a kilometre away. No Sasquatch had ever been captured, so it had to have some kind of adaptations to protect it from predators.

"I wonder if Sasquatches are like bears?" whispered Sam, thinking back to yesterday's scary encounter.

"I don't think so. It's big like a bear, but that doesn't look like fur all over it."

"No," agreed Sam. "It looks more like hair." He stared more closely at the creature's face and neck. "Some of the hair's grey, too, isn't it?"

"I think so. Maybe it's an old Sasquatch, like my moushoom and your grandpa."

"Maybe. I don't think I want to try making a noise and walking right past it, like we did with the bear."

"Me neither."

The Sasquatch turned its head from side to side, but remained motionless. It seemed to be thinking, or perhaps it was confused about something.

"Sasquatches could be more like apes and orang-utans," suggested Sam, remembering some of the information he'd found on the Internet while Taneal was writing her story this afternoon. "Scientists think it may be related to an ancient creature called the *Gigantopithecus*. That was a kind of huge ape that lived at the same time as early man."

"But there aren't any apes here."

"They think maybe we just haven't dug up any of their bones yet," said Sam. "They're always discovering new kinds of dinosaurs and other extinct creatures."

"So what are you supposed to do when you see an ape?"

"When Grandpa and I spent the day taking pictures at the zoo, we talked to some of the zoo keepers. They said you should never act scared with apes and chimps and orang-utans, but you shouldn't pretend to be friendly either, like you would with a person. No smiling or reaching out to touch."

"Who would do that anyway?" scoffed Taneal.

Sam shrugged and stared glumly at his camera.

Above them the sun had nearly reached the horizon on its downward path across the sky. "Maybe we could just wait until after dark and sneak away," suggested Taneal.

The last thing Sam wanted to do was stay crouched behind this tree in the dark. Would they even be able to find their way back to the cabin without light? "What does your moushoom tell you to do around other animals?"

Taneal's answer was quick, as if she'd heard it repeated many times. "Stay a long way back and respect their space."

Suddenly, the Sasquatch took two short, stealthy strides towards them. Sam and Taneal ducked even lower behind the tree, hoping against hope that, if the creature couldn't see them, it wouldn't smell them or sense them some other way instead.

"What about if you're too close to respect their space?" hissed Sam. If he were the Sasquatch he was sure he'd think these two humans were already too close.

"Well, my auntie had a moose right outside her front door one time. She just waited until it got tired of standing there and went away."

"Yeah, well, if we were behind a door instead of an old bit of tree, maybe I wouldn't be so scared."

"Me neither."

When they risked another look, the Sasquatch had closed the distance between them by another metre. It was so close now they could see that it walked very much like a person, and not at all like animals such as bears.

"How can you tell if an animal is going to attack to protect itself?" asked Sam. "Maybe we shouldn't be worried?"

"Bears stand up and sniff the air, like that one did yesterday. Then, if they're afraid you might be dangerous, they might make a fake charge at you – to scare you away."

Sam shuddered at the idea of a creature whose head would touch the ceiling of most houses charging at him, even if it was fake!

Now the Sasquatch was bending, touching its hand to the ground . . . It stood up, swung its arm out to the side and . . .

Thump!

"A rock! It's throwing rocks at us! Duck, Taneal!"

"I guess we know one way that Sasquatches protect themselves," hissed Sam, sticking his head back up to see what was happening.

A half-metre-long dried branch hit their fallen tree with enough force to shake it from end to end. The creature might be old, but it had plenty of strength left!

It was bending again now, searching for another missile. Then it made another call, this time not so loud, and more like an anguished cry. Was it trying to tell them something?

"What do you think?" whispered Taneal. "Is it male or female?"

"Does it matter?"

"Well, didn't the Internet say that males were much stronger?"

One story they'd read had said that a male Sasquatch had thrown a barrel of diesel fuel, weighing more than 200 kilograms, as easily as if it were a giant ball.

Ideas rolled one after the other through Sam's head. How did you escape from a Sasquatch? Run? No, that just didn't seem wise. Hiding hadn't worked either. He couldn't think of a single thing that humans possessed to protect themselves against something so big, besides their intelligence. And he was beginning to think that Sasquatches were pretty smart, too.

"I don't think we're safe here," he whispered. "So what if we just back away, slowly, keeping our eyes on it, so it thinks we're not afraid. Do you think that might work?"

"Who's not afraid?"

Sam tried to smile. "Maybe it's like dealing with a bully. If they realise you're afraid of them, they keep picking on you more and more."

"Maybe," said Taneal doubtfully. "But, when other wild animals decide you're not a threat, they usually leave you alone. So, if the Sasquatch thinks we're retreating, maybe it won't throw anything else at us."

A surge of adrenalin ran through Sam. He couldn't just cower here and wait for whatever to happen. He needed to act! He grabbed the rough surface of the fallen tree and pulled himself up slowly, so as not to startle the creature. He also wanted to be able to dive for cover if another projectile came flying through the air.

"Let's just keep moving back until we get to our bikes," said Sam out of the corner of his mouth. "Then jump on and ride away."

"Okay." Slowly, Taneal got to her feet, too, and soon she was standing beside him.

And now, for the first time, Sam realised that this was his last chance to get a picture of the

Sasquatch. Could he risk stopping to focus the camera and click a picture? No. The creature was much too close!

Sucking in a giant breath of air, Sam turned the dial on the camera to video mode and turned it on. Seeing what he was doing, Taneal did the same with hers. Then, holding the cameras in front of them, they began to move backwards.

One step back. Two steps. Three.

"Owwwww," spluttered Taneal, then slapped her hand over her mouth to hold back a scream. After a moment, her words came out in little gasps. "My ankle, I think I twisted my ankle!"

The Sasquatch bent and ran its hands over the ground. Did it think the muffled scream was a challenge? But now it had straightened up again, without another missile to throw. Had it somehow understood that Taneal was hurt?

"Are you all right?" whispered Sam

"Maybe." She put some weight on her foot. "Ouch! I'm sure it'll be okay in a minute. Let's just go slow."

How could they possibly get away now? If the Sasquatch rushed them, they'd be at its mercy.

Taneal would never be able to run fast enough and he couldn't go without her.

The Sasquatch held its position and Sam saw the creature's chest heave and fall – was it afraid, too?

One step back. Two steps. Five steps. The videos rolled on.

Now the ground behind Sam began to feel uneven again. Could Taneal manage? His left foot brushed over the surface, hit something soft and yielding – a plant perhaps – then found firm ground. Now his right foot. He kept a firm grip on Taneal's arm and, with his help, she followed him step by step.

In front of them, the Sasquatch remained frozen, as if it truly were a relic from a long-past ice age.

Sam risked a moment's pause to glance down at the camera. He pushed the button to end the video recording and turned the selection dial to automatic picture taking. There wouldn't be any time to adjust the settings.

"Leave yours on video," he whispered to Taneal.

They took another step backwards.

Snap!

They were at least thirty metres away.

Snap! Snap!

The Sasquatch continued to stare at Sam and Taneal, but the only things that moved were its eyes.

Scarlet, carmine, amaranth, orchid and cranberry began to fill the western sky as the sun became a glowing ball of colour. Sunset.

Looking backwards now, they hobbled another half-dozen metres, until Taneal fell to the ground beside her bike.

Sam glanced back, expecting to see the Sasquatch in the distance, but there was nothing there. Where had it gone?

"It just disappeared! One moment I was watching it and the next it was gone!" Sam felt relieved, but sad, too.

Taneal rubbed her ankle and stared glumly down at the road.

"Maybe somebody can come for us," said Sam, pulling Grandma's cellphone out of his waist bag. He flipped it open, but nothing happened.

"Is it on?" Taneal asked.

"I thought so." Sam pressed the on button again. Nothing. "I guess the battery's dead."

Taneal groaned.

"Can you ride your bike?"

The trees that lined the road ahead of them were dark, ominous blobs.

"I'll try."

Chills of fear still chased each other down his spine but, as each push of the pedal took them further away from the creature, all Sam could think about was the pictures. It had been dusk. Would the videos and pictures show the Sasquatch or just a dark, shapeless blob?

TEN

That morning, the last part of the trail through the bush had been a squishy, muddy mess, but now the ground was hard and dry. Still, Taneal found the way without hesitation, even in the dark.

A raven cawed and flew away from its perch with a flutter and flap of midnight wings.

"We're . . . almost . . . there," gasped Taneal through gritted teeth.

At the resort, people sat outside the cabins, enjoying the cooler evening air. There was still enough light to pick out their friendly expressions as Sam shouted, "Hello."

Taneal called out, too. "Hello!"

When they got back to the cabin, Grandpa was leaning over the porch railing, watching for them. "Did you get . . . good pictures?"

Sam dropped his bike beside the cabin and leapt over to help Taneal get off hers. "We sure did, Grandpa!"

"What's wrong, Taneal? Have you hurt yourself?" said Grandma, hurrying down the steps to take Taneal's other arm.

"Come on, Taneal, sit down and let's see what you've done to yourself," said Dad, pulling up one of the brown plastic outdoor chairs.

"I just twisted my ankle a little. It doesn't hurt too much."

"A sprained ankle, probably," said Grandma, running her hands carefully over Taneal's foot. "There's a little swelling already."

"It's all right, really it is. The most important thing is . . . " Taneal turned to Sam, giving him the chance to tell everyone.

"We saw the Sasquatch up close and took lots of pictures and video," he blurted, smiling gratefully at Taneal.

Grandpa reached for Sam's camera as Taneal began to tell them all about it. "It was so tall. The most amazing animal I've ever seen!"

"A *Sasquatch*?" Dad shook his head. "Sam, don't you remember your grandfather and me telling you there was to be no more creature hunting? You were specifically told not to go back to where you'd found those tracks."

"But we didn't go hunting the creature, we went just where we said we would, down to the boat ramp to take pictures at sunset."

"We *did*," insisted Taneal, handing her camera to a concerned-looking Grandpa. "We rode our bikes up the road to the boat ramp place, then we walked a little way out to a fallen tree. But we were right by the ramp, just like we promised."

"If the cellphone had worked you could have come and seen us there," said Sam, unzipping the camera bag and pulling out the phone. "I tried to call you to come get us when Taneal twisted her ankle, but the battery was dead."

"Oh, my goodness," said Grandma. "I guess it needs charging. I'm so sorry."

Grandpa was pulling himself closer on his walker. "But what about the pictures?" he asked. "Are you sure it was a . . . Sasquatch?"

Taneal grinned. "One hundred per cent

absolutely without a doubt positively for sure."

"Okay, let's download . . . what you have." With the cameras dangling from his walker, he shuffled slowly across the deck and opened the cabin door, letting out a waft of savoury pasta sauce that had lingered since dinner.

All at once, Sam felt hungry again. It seemed like a very long time since dinner.

At the computer, Grandpa downloaded the images from his old camera and everyone gathered around, finding places to sit on the couch or on the floor. Sam curled up right at Grandpa's knee, so he wouldn't miss a thing.

One by one, the photos sailed from the camera to the laptop.

"Just wait until you hear the sounds the Sasquatch makes!" said Taneal, but her attempts to demonstrate didn't sound nearly as scary as the real thing.

"It screamed like that?" asked Dad. "With a range of different sounds?"

Taneal nodded.

"It really did, Dad," said Sam. "We both made videos, so you should hear all the different noises, except for the first few, when I was too scared to turn on the camera."

Grandma shook her head. "I'm not sure I really want to see these videos and think about what could have happened."

"It's all right, Grandma. We tried to respect its space and understand what it wanted." Sam watched the laptop monitor. The last image had flown across and landed.

"Ready?" said Grandpa, glancing around. "This may be your greatest . . . photo shoot ever, Sam."

He certainly hoped so!

Grandpa clicked on the first video.

A close-up of the bark of the fallen tree they'd hidden behind was the first thing Sam saw. Then, as the camera pointed higher, there it was! The Sasquatch, outlined against the darkening sky!

"Look at that!" shouted Dad in amazement. "It's a real live Sasquatch!"

On the video soundtrack, the creature began its unearthly howl and Grandma gasped. "What a horrible sound."

Sam glanced up at Grandpa, but he couldn't

tell what he was thinking. "It was more terrible then than it is now."

"This isn't quite what I expected when we planned a holiday in northern Saskatchewan," said Dad, shaking his head.

Sam wished the video would end so he could see if the photographs had turned out. He closed his eyes and imagined one of his pictures on the front page of the newspaper, along with his name.

Click-click. Grandpa closed the video and opened the first picture of the Sasquatch. There it was! The hairy body. The dangling arms. The strange expression on its face.

Nobody said anything as Grandpa clicked through the images, one by one. They could be improved with software adjustments, but each was already clear and sharp and vivid enough to see the Sasquatch clearly.

"You've done it, Sam," cried Grandpa. "The photograph . . . of the century."

Grandpa went through the pictures twice more, while everyone watched, then they all watched the video from Taneal's camera, too. The grown-ups seemed to be struggling to come to terms with the fact that Sam and Taneal had been in such danger and managed to survive without being hurt. They all seemed to think of the Sasquatch as a wild animal.

But Sam didn't feel like it was a wild animal. Not something you'd put in the zoo. He couldn't stand the thought of the Sasquatch behind bars, as if it had done something wrong and been sent to prison.

"I'm hungry," he announced, knowing that would break up the party while Grandma went looking for something to eat. He wanted time to think about what would happen when people saw his pictures. They were so clear and vivid – absolute proof that the Sasquatch was real.

He tried to get Taneal's attention, to ask her what she thought he should do, but Grandma was keeping her busy.

Meanwhile, Grandpa was putting a DVD into the disk drive to backup the photos before he shut the laptop down. He'd always taught Sam to save the original images immediately, so they didn't accidentally get deleted or changed. The original was the most important photo, even if it was improved by graphics software later, because it alone held the exact information captured the moment it was snapped.

"Taneal, I'd better drive you home before your dad starts to worry about you," said Dad.

"Thanks, Mr Christos." Taneal turned to Sam. "See you in the morning, Sam?"

Sam nodded. "Hope your ankle feels better by then." He'd have to wait until tomorrow to ask her what she thought he should do about the Sasquatch pictures.

"Well, if not, we can have another writing day inside," said Sam's dad cheerily. "Maybe Sam will join us, too."

"I guess I could write about the Sasquatch, as well as just taking its picture," said Sam, as Taneal hopped through the door on Dad's arm, calling her goodbyes. "See you tomorrow."

By the time Dad returned, Grandma had some crackers and cheese ready and Sam offered to get the plates. He knew that, as soon as he sat still, someone would have more questions for him.

Grandpa had his snack in front of the computer, where he was working on the best of the photos and Sam sat beside him, watching the creature's grey hair become clearer as Grandpa zoomed in on the picture to sharpen the contrast. Sam glanced from Grandpa's sloped shoulders to the creature's – he was sure it was old, too. Maybe even older than Grandpa.

How long had this Sasquatch lived without being caught, or even seen, by humans? The one protective adaptation the Sasquatch seemed to have was its ability to disappear after it had been sighted. Maybe it truly did slip into another reality – one that was safer than earth. Sam certainly hoped so.

He went to bed as soon as he could, saying he was tired, which was true enough, but he tossed and turned in bed instead of sleeping. As soon as the world found out about the Sasquatch, scientists would try to catch it, study it, do tests on it. They'd put it in a laboratory or a zoo forever.

Sam couldn't bear to think about it, so he watched the moonlight glow through the window over his bed and remembered his mother reading him his favourite story about saying goodnight to the moon. Was the Sasquatch looking up at their moon now, or was he in some other world?

Soon Sam could be famous. Newspapers would want to print his photos of the Sasquatch. TV stations and the Internet would want to show his video. Scientists and newscasters would ask him a million questions about the Sasquatch – how it behaved and what he'd seen.

Then the rubberneckers would come by the carload and busload to Land of the Loon and Anglin Lake and Prince Albert National Park. They'd search everywhere for the Sasquatch. They'd trample over the prairie, drive quad bikes through the forest, zoom motor boats across the lakes, looking in every bay and hollow they could find. Just as they had with the crop circles, they'd keep coming back, again and again and again.

Even if the Sasquatch had slipped through to another dimension, the park would never be the same. Sam didn't want that to happen.

Now another thought came into his mind and he shot up in bed. Had this all been like the Big Man that Taneal had talked about? Had the Sasquatch appeared to give him some kind of a message? What could it have been?

He tried to remember every moment of the encounter, but the only thing that popped into his head was the image of the Sasquatch, standing as still as a statue, almost as if it were posing for his pictures.

Was that it? Had this old Sasquatch come to make sure he took the pictures that would make him famous?

That just didn't feel right.

What else then? Why had he taken the pictures anyway? Was it just to get famous? To show Grandpa what a good photographer he had become?

Sam thought about Grandpa. Taking pictures with him had been the very best part of their annual holiday. Even this year, when Grandpa couldn't do a lot after the stroke, it had still been the best part. Each day, Grandpa had been here to see his pictures, pick out his best shots and help him to learn how to use software to improve them. Grandpa had even given him his back-up camera, so he could learn to take better pictures. Despite the stroke, they were still sharing lots of things and having fun – it was just different fun.

The more he thought about it, the more Sam realised that all these years of taking pictures with Grandpa on holidays had been about him and Grandpa, not about either of them becoming a famous photographer. They'd had a great time even when the best picture of the day was just of an everyday frog or rabbit. And each year they'd sent out their Christmas calendar of photos to share with all their friends.

Maybe the reason Grandpa had never won a photography contest was that he'd never bothered to enter one.

The Sasquatch hadn't appeared to make Sam famous for his photography. The Sasquatch had come to help him understand that pictures are a way to remember and share, even when everything has changed.

Whatever happened in the future, Sam promised himself that these precious images would remain where they belonged – with him and his family. The rest of the world would never see the Sasquatch. Or, at least, not through his pictures.